It's Hard to Tell You How I Feel

It's Hard to Tell You How I Feel

Helping Children
Express and
Understand
Their Feelings

Richard L. Krebs

AUGSBURG
Publishing House
Minneapolis

IT'S HARD TO TELL YOU HOW I FEEL

Scripture quotations unless otherwise noted are from the Revised Standard Version of the Bible, copyright 1946, 1952, and 1971 by the Division of Christian Education of the National Council of Churches.

Photos: Strix Pix, 14, 27, 45, 91, 122; Paul Buddle, 21, 27; Paul Schrock, 37; Judy Burr, 52; Jean-Claude Lejeune, 62; Vivienne della Grotta, 71, 86, 97, 115.

MANUFACTURED IN THE UNITED STATES OF AMERICA

For my own children,
Carol, Randy, Laurie, and Robbie,
who have told me much about how children feel

Contents

Preface

I sit in his room waiting for him to die. He is old, and life is too painful to sustain. Breathing, moving, even thinking are too much now. So he and I wait together for his release.

He is my wife's grandfather, and I call him "George," but he has been like a grandfather to me. We have loved one another. Although the word "love" has never been used, we both know how the other feels.

When in earlier days we talked about corn and cabbage and beans in the garden, a garden we have shared for many years, the feeling that passed between us was one of love.

As I would recount what each of his four great-grandchildren had done on that day, the feeling that passed between us was love.

When we reminisced about his years as a farmer, the hard times and the good ones, the feeling that passed between us was one of love.

George is weak and old now and he needs to die, but the love that he has shared with me and with my wife, or with our four children, or his two daughters, or his wife Bertha—that love is as strong as ever. In fact, as George has grown weaker, the love he has given us, and we, him, seems to have become even more clear and strong. It is as though in approaching death, love has been freed from everything that used to capture and dilute it.

This book will speak of love, but it will also speak of anger and pain and hatred. For it is a book about feelings, what feelings are and how we and our children can handle them.

The book will speak of the many feelings we have during a lifetime. Feelings expressed and un-expressed. Feelings understood and feelings never quite grasped. Feelings that carry us along and those that bring us up short. Feelings that we treasure and feelings that we try, sometimes with great effort, to forget.

But St. Paul was right. The greatest, the most enduring, the most powerful feeling of them all is truly love. May love, God's love, guide you now as you read this book.

1

What Is a Feeling?

Jody sat on the porch swing. The day was hot, but there was a breeze. Here on the side porch with its vines and trellises it was always cool and shady.

He knew that the tomato patch still needed to be weeded, but he thought his mother wouldn't mind if he sat for a while after the noonday meal.

"Biscuits and gravy," he thought. "My favorite." And in his mind he could see the dark brown beef gravy with small pieces of meat floating in it. The biscuits were day-old, but with gravy on them their faded freshness didn't matter.

"Jody, Jody," his mother called from the door. "What you doing out here?"

"Nothing, Ma," Jody replied.

"You haven't forgotten the hoeing that has to be done, have you?"

"No, Ma. I'm going to get to it as soon as my dinner settles in."

"All right if I join you for a few minutes?" his mother asked, sitting down opposite him on an old faded-green wooden rocker.

"That's fine, Ma. Cool here, isn't it?"

"Yes. I just can't face those dishes yet. The kitchen gets so hot this time of day. I wish the porch continued around the back so's it would shade the kitchen. Well, maybe one of these days . . . , " she said, her voice trailing off.

The two sat quietly. The rocker and swing creaking were the only sounds.

Jody's mother came out of her reverie first. "Jody. Jody Powell, what's going on in that head of yours?" she said looking at her twelve-year-old son. "What are you thinking about?"

Jody shifted embarrassedly on the swing. "Nothing much, Ma."

"Now don't tell me you're thinking about tomato plants. You looked much too far away for that. What are you thinking about?"

"Well, when you got to talking about the back porch, it made me think of Dad, and how I'll bet he would've built that porch for you if he were still here. He always wanted things to be good for you. And I, well . . . , " but the tears that were building up in his throat got in the way of his words and he couldn't finish the sentence.

"Yes, I suspect you're right, Jody. I suspect your Daddy would've built that porch if he had lived." Mrs. Powell's own eyes glazed over and they both were quiet for a few minutes.

"Jody, I know things haven't been easy for you these last two years," Mrs. Powell continued, her composure regained. "I know sometimes I seem to take all you do around here for granted. It's just, well, it's just that I'm busy and I never have been too good with words. But I want you to know how proud I am of you."

Jody could feel his face flushing, and his eyes were beginning to sting. "I'll just get on those tomatoes now," he said as he walked toward the porch steps.

Mrs. Powell touched his hand as Jody passed her. "So proud," she said softly, and a tear ran slowly down her right cheek.

FEELINGS

Jody Powell is not very different from most of us when we were his age, reluctant to speak of our feelings, uncertain about how to put them into words.

But what is this thing that Jody is having trouble talking about? What is a *feeling*? Not a dictionary definition of it, but a practical one, a definition we can get hold of and wrestle with. Suppose we try the following: "A *feeling* is something inside that ought to be outside."

All of us have feelings. Their range and quality are endless. They cascade through us like a river— rapidly twisting and turning, then running quietly, peacefully. Often they change from minute to

minute. At other times they may last for hours, even days.

"Isn't what you're talking about a *mood?*" you ask. "Are a *mood* and a *feeling* the same thing?"

No, not quite. A mood is like a feeling minus thought and words. A mood also is more private and personal than a feeling. When a mood comes out, it is likely to be without our awareness or even against our will.

"I didn't mean to be grouchy," we say apologetically. "I've been in a bad mood all week. "

A mood, even a good mood, is usually vague. When we want to share it with someone else, we have to change it into a feeling. We have to name it, label it, describe it in order to share it.

Moods are at the root of many feelings, but the two are not the same. We need to use our minds to turn a mood into a feeling.

"Oh, I see what you mean. A feeling is more like an idea than it is like a mood. A feeling is a type of idea that we give a name to so that we can tell someone else about it."

No. No, it's not quite true that a feeling and an idea are the same either. An idea doesn't have a bodily referent. An idea is something in our heads. A feeling seems to demand more from us than just thought. It effects all of us, mind and body.

HANDLING FEELINGS

Let's go back to Jody for a minute. He's outside now in the tomato patch. The sun is warm against his skin. His stomach is full from lunch. There are a few sweatbees buzzing near his ears. He could pay attention to any of these stimuli and turn them into a feeling, but his attention is focused on the lump in his throat. It's a little smaller now than it was when he was on the porch with his mother. Then it felt so big and brittle that he thought something would surely break inside. Now the lump is a little smaller and a bit less brittle, but it is still prominent enough that it is hard for him to ignore it.

Jody might decide to handle the lump in his throat by saying to himself, "There's that lump again. I get it every time we talk about Dad. I wish it would go away. Maybe if I just don't pay any attention to it. . . . That's what I'll do, I'll just forget about it."

And you know, that'll probably work.

I know psychologists aren't supposed to say things like that. Feelings are supposed to be expressed and understood, not smothered or repressed. But the fact is that all of us smother feelings. We have to. We have to because if we paid attention to them all, we wouldn't get anything else done, since there are scores of potential feelings inside us all the time.

We also have to ignore feelings because sometimes we just can't share a particular feeling. The timing isn't right, or the setting isn't conducive, so we shift our attention to something else. Sure enough, most of the time, if we check back later on the feeling, it's gone.

Later in the book we'll look at those feelings that don't go away so easily, and we'll look at the advantages of expressing them. But for now it's not a bad idea to remind ourselves that one of the characteristics of feelings is that they *do go away*.

Did you ever think about *where* those feelings go? Are they perhaps like an odor that dissipates until it's so diluted that we can't smell it anymore? Or like a sound that reverberates and echoes until our ears can no longer sense it? When they go, do feelings simply disappear without a trace?

No, because if they disappeared without a trace, then Jody wouldn't be thinking about *that* lump in the throat as though it were familiar. He might be thinking about *a* lump, but the lump that was in his throat this afternoon felt like the lump that had been there many times before. Even though his lump came and went, it was somehow still the same, like a friend with new clothes on, or a car with a new paint job. The feeling may be a little different each time it comes; but, at the center, it's still the same.

Yes, feelings go away, but they leave a trace somewhere in those incredibly complex minds of ours, a trace that allows them to return or to be called back, so that we can reexperience them and reexamine them even many years later.

DEFINITION OF A FEELING

Feelings are funny things—changeable yet very resistant to eradication. A feeling, Jody's feeling or ours, is something that involves a bodily sensation and thought, is likely to fade away when we don't pay attention to it, and yet is capable of returning instantaneously even many years later. It also is something that pushes for expression. We may decide not to express a feeling, or we may find that even though we want to express it, we can't. But a feeling always has a degree of insistence about it, that is like *something inside trying to get out.*

We'll be back to Jody later to see what happens to his lump-in-the-throat feeling, but it might be helpful if we were to spend a bit more time looking at feelings in general and why they are so important to us—especially why it's so important to talk about them.

2

The Importance of Talking About Feelings

If feelings are something inside that ought to come out, why don't they? And more to the point of this book, why do children have trouble expressing their feelings?

CHILDREN EXPRESSING FEELINGS

To get to the second question first, little children don't have any trouble expressing their feelings. They do have trouble, a lot of trouble, *talking* about their feelings, but *expressing* them? No, no trouble at all.

"I hate you, Mommy! You're mean and ugly! Mud pies are prettier than you!"

"This chocolate ice cream is yummy, delicious."

If feelings—strong, changing, even contradictory feelings—tumble out of young children with ease, then why do things get jammed up? Why, when you ask most school-age children how they feel about someone or something, do they mumble, "I don't know"? What happens to that tumbling preschool brook of feelings? Where does it go?

UNDERGROUND FEELINGS

It goes underground—frequently so far underground that the child can no longer touch it. They may in fact even forget that it is there. The remaining dry stream bed, the last remaining trace of a feeling, may be difficult to find. The school-age child's "I don't know" is not usually a way to avoid confronting something unpleasant, but simply a matter of fact. School-age children simply aren't as in touch with their feelings as preschoolers are.

People who idealize children sometimes get teary-eyed when they watch a bubbling three-year-old turn into a staid six-year-old. "Isn't it a shame what's happened to Cheryl? She used to be so open, and now she's *so* quiet. Those schools with all their rules and regimentations. They squeeze the life out of children." But do they?

Are schools really to blame for the flattening of the feelings of school-age children? While many theories have been suggested to explain the fact that school-age children are less expressive of feelings than younger children—socialization, repres-

sion, reinforcement—there's another possible explanation, one that makes equal sense and doesn't have the negative connotations of most of the other theories. This explanation suggests that children's feelings go underground because they have to.

TOO CLOSE TO TELL

Have you ever been in the house for a long time, especially during the winter when the windows were closed? The smells of cooking, smoking, and the dog, build up slowly, imperceptibly. Then you go outside for a few hours. As you come back into the house, you catch your breath and say aloud, "My gosh, it stinks in here!" You hadn't noticed the smells while you were living with them. In order to know they were there, you had to get away from them and then come back again.

Small children's feelings are like the smells in the closed house. Their feelings are so much a part of them that they are not noticed. Young children and their feelings are a single unit, unrecognized, simply there.

By way of explanation, let's go back to the "Mommy, I hate you" routine of a young child. If you have escaped the seething anger of a two-year-old, you are a unique individual (or more likely you just have not been around a two-year-old during limit-setting time). For the angry response of a two-year-old who has been told "no" is as predictable as the rising of the sun. If you were to ask a screaming two-year-old if he were angry at his mommy, he might well respond "No."

"But didn't you just say you hated her?"

"I do hate her. I wish she was dead!"

"So doesn't that mean you're angry with her for telling you that you couldn't have ice cream?"

"No, I *hate* her!"

Exasperating? It can be if you look at the young child's expression of feeling from an adult point of view. The problem is not that a two-year-old does not understand the word "angry," rather a two-year-old child simply *is* his feelings. Feelings are not something a two-year-old has; they are something a two-year-old is. When two-year-olds say, "I hate you," they *are* hatred. They *are* fury. They can't talk about their feelings—they can't compare their feelings with one another, because they and their feelings are one.

THE NEED FOR DISTANCE

In order for children to talk about their feelings there has to be some distance between them and their feelings, and that's why feelings go underground about the time they go to school. There is a natural, necessary process going, one that will result in a child's being able to talk about feelings rather than simply expressing them. This process will also create the option to feel a feeling, but not express it, and to elaborate, dissect, and truly understand a feeling even if it is very subtle and complicated.

WHY TALK ABOUT FEELINGS?

In this book we will be looking together at the process that creates an emotionally mature human being. But before we go any further, we will take some time to think together about why talking about feelings is important. How does the ability to talk about our feelings make us, or help to make us, emotionally mature?

I've committed the last twenty years of my life to understanding feelings—my own and other people's. When I first began my training as a psychologist, I worked for a time at a private psychiatric hospital as an attendant. I was assigned to a locked, active-treatment ward. There was one man on the ward, I'll call him Mr. Norman, who never talked. In fact, he didn't do much of anything. He ate his breakfast, and he sat. He ate his lunch, and he sat. He ate his dinner, sat, and then went to bed. Occasionally he walked around the ward for a few minutes. Several times a week I took him to another part of the building to see his psychiatrist.

Then one day he got in line when the other patients were waiting to go out for a walk around the grounds. "Mr. Norman, are you coming with us?" I asked.

I don't know if I was ignoring the obvious or hoping that he might respond verbally, but he simply stood quietly in line until the door was unlocked and then walked out with the rest of us and around the garden.

Every day after that Mr. Norman lined up with

us, and I continued to try to engage him in conversation. One day as he was sitting under a tree, I sat down with him and asked what he was doing. To my surprise he said, "I'm writing a book."

"What kind of a book?" I asked, barely containing my excitement.

"A children's book. About a horse," he replied.

They were his first words in many months, and they were followed by others. I don't want you to get the idea that Mr. Norman turned into a lively conversationalist, but he did occasionally talk to me, and I learned that he was finally talking to his psychiatrist.

Several years later I saw Mr. Norman again, and this time he was walking quietly, contentedly outside a large apartment building many miles from the hospital.

Before he came to the hospital, Mr. Norman's feelings had not only gone underground, they had gone so far underground that they were not expressed or talked about at all. He had become catatonic, unresponsive, a zombie. Only as he got back into a relationship did the spring of his feelings that had dried up begin to put forth water again.

Mr. Norman is an extreme example of what happens to unexpressed, untalked about feelings. I never did know much about what had caused him to become so withdrawn, but there was no question that the way back to mental and emotional wholeness lay in his getting that stream of feelings back up to the surface again. I've always been glad that

I played a part in helping to open up the spring that fed that stream.

Most people who don't express or talk about their feelings end up in far less difficulty than Mr. Norman. They have psychosomatic problems—headaches, high blood pressure, general fatigue—but they don't become psychotic. Still others become neurotic—depressed, anxious, confused. Many simply don't function as well as they might. All because they don't express or talk about their feelings?

How could feelings be so powerful? How could expressing or not expressing them make such a major difference in a person? Psychotic, neurotic, psychosomatic—can all those terrible states really be caused by something as simple as not expressing feelings? Does that mean that to be emotionally healthy we have to express our feelings—no matter how antisocial or obnoxious those feelings might be?

Well, only partly. There is another option to the expression of a feeling, and that's the possibility of feeling the feeling, understanding it, but not letting it out directly. It's sort of like letting the feeling out through the top of one's head, rather than out one's mouth.

THE INDIRECT EXPRESSION
OF FEELINGS

Let me try another example, one that points to this second, less direct way of handling a feeling. Most of the people I see in my private practice are having trouble expressing feelings. Either they

impulsively or destructively let feelings fly, or they repress them so completely that they are not even aware of them. They are husbands who beat their wives, parents who verbally and physically abuse their children, or people whose feelings are so locked up and distorted that they can only get out in physical symptoms or vague depression or anxiety.

Roland Roth is such a person. He is a thirty-year-old husband and father of two. He teaches school. He is a respected member of the community. And he is very depressed.

His depression started after his second child, a daughter, was born. He couldn't sleep. He started losing weight. He felt sad and lethargic, but neither he nor his physician could find anything wrong.

There was nothing in his current life that he could put his finger on. He liked his work and loved his wife and children—but something was wrong.

As we began to work together, I learned that Roland had grown up as the oldest child of a Protestant minister. It was expected that he would be a good boy, and he was. In fact, he was *too* good. He never did anything wrong, at least nothing that he could recall. He was a model child.

When he was in his second year of college, his mother died, and Roland fell apart. He nearly flunked out of school, but with some counseling he managed to get through the year.

Now, ten years later, he felt he was back at the same spot he had been in college: depressed, uncertain, feeling like giving up, but he had no clear excuse this time. Ten years ago he could blame his mother's death; now there was nothing to blame except his daughter's birth. That couldn't be it, or could it?

As we dug back deeper into Roland's past, we discovered that when his younger sister had been born, his mother had been very ill, so ill that she nearly died. She was kept in the hospital for several weeks after the baby was born and remained in bed for many weeks thereafter. For several months Roland, who was only two and a half, had virtually no contact with his mother.

Session after session Roland tried to dig back into his memory for clues about his current depression. Finally, one afternoon we broke through a "wall."

"You know, Dr. Krebs, I can always remember trying to be good. I don't mean that I just didn't want to get caught doing things that were bad, I mean I *always wanted to be good*. You know the verse in the Bible, 'You must be perfect'? Well, I was, or at least I tried to be, but I was always scared."

"Of what?" I asked.

Roland was quiet for a while, and then tears began to trickle down his cheeks, "Scared, scared that my mommy would go away again if I was bad."

"Did you really think she went away because you were bad?"

"I guess so . . . ," he replied thoughtfully. There was a long silence, and then he continued. "I just had a picture, like a film clip in my head. I'm beating on my mommy's belly. I'm mad at her. I don't want a little baby brother or sister. I want my mommy." His voice sounded child-like, and the tears were flowing profusely now.

That memory of the hurt, angry, frightened little boy did not immediately evaporate Roland's depression. But his tears were the beginning, the beginning of an outlet for long-censored feelings, for unreasonable demands for perfection. Feelings that had been trying to get out for over a quarter of a century had finally found a path to the outside.

They came out not in angry denunciation of his mother, who was long since dead, nor in unreasonable recriminations toward himself. Rather, they came out in sad, gentle thoughts and memories that recognized that no one was to blame. Roland came to understand that his current feelings of depression were a second chance to deal with the feelings that he had not been able to handle as a little boy. Feelings that had been restimulated by the birth of his second child, a little girl, like his own sister. Feelings that had been brought a little closer to the surface when his first child, a son, had been born, a kind of second Roland, and now had flowed back to consciousness with the birth of his second child two years later.

The birth of his own two children had created a situation that was parallel to the circumstances that existed when he was two and a half: a little boy followed two years later by a little girl. Roland had been given a second chance, a chance to feel those old feelings again, a chance to build a new life that could include imperfection.

UNDERSTANDING A FEELING

Roland worked many months in therapy to uncover his old feelings and then to put a new life together, but he could not have gotten the new start if those old feelings had not gotten out. Feelings are like that. Sooner or later, someway or other, they just have to come out.

Those of you who have been in psychotherapy know what I'm talking about. If you have no experience with psychotherapy, you still may know what I'm talking about. Sitting down with a friend or your spouse and being able to understand what has been wrong between you is very similar to what goes on in psychotherapy. A slight, a misunderstanding, a difference of opinion had divided the two of you. When you both understood what was wrong, the tense feeling that filled the air between you was gone. Understanding a feeling can make an immense difference in us as individuals and in our relationships with other people.

Feelings can get out by being expressed, but they can also get out by being understood. Sometimes, especially when the feelings are strong or negative or the person for whom they were meant is no longer around, then the best way, sometimes the only way, is to let them get out by understanding them.

We've been focusing primarily on feelings of

adults, but children have feelings, too, feelings that are complex, difficult to express and to understand. With this background on the importance of feelings, suppose we now turn our attention to the feelings of children. The person who is going to help us understand children and their feelings is Dr. Charlotte Ellinwood. I'd like to introduce her to you now.

3

Children
and Their Feelings

I first met Charlotte Ellinwood nearly twenty years ago. I was in training as a psychotherapist, and she was the child-therapy instructor at the University of Chicago's Counseling Center.

The one word that best described Charlotte was "simple." Simple in dress and speech. Simple and straightforward in her approach to the troubled children with whom she worked. Simple and helpful in trying to explain the complexities of child therapy to us, her students.

Several years later, when she asked if I would help her with a study she was doing on the development of feelings in children, I was pleased to be able to partially repay the debt I owed her for helping me to become at least a moderately successful child therapist.

As I began to read over the rating scales that she planned to use to understand how children talked about their feelings, I was impressed by the simple elegance of her propositions. In fact I was so impressed that I said a very unscientific, almost blasphemous thing. "Charlotte," I said to her, "if your data don't work out, if they don't prove what you're trying to find, throw the data away and collect new data because these scales *have* to be right."

The rating scales were logical, almost beautiful in their simplicity, and like most *truly* simple things sure to be correct. (When I say truly simple, I don't mean naive or simple-minded. I mean truly simple in the sense of the simplicity of the double-helix model of the DNA molecule, simple in the way that a crystal is simple, or simple in the way that love is simple.) And so while normally a scientist is supposed to be led by facts rather than theory, in the case of Charlotte Ellinwood's work, I was convinced that her theory ought to take precedence even over facts.

Fortunately, as the study progressed, it became clear that theory and facts were going to support each other, so Charlotte never had to choose between them.

THE FACTS ABOUT CHILDREN'S FEELINGS

A number of years ago a Swiss psychologist, Jean Piaget, began watching and listening to children. Most of the time he talked to and listened to his own children. Sometimes he studied other children too, but what Piaget did that people before him had not done was that he *really* listened to children, and he let what the children said determine the categories he used to try to understand their world.

Piaget found that the world of a child, especially a young child, is very different from the world of an adult. Categories that we use without thinking —inside vs. outside, my point of view vs. your point of view, animate vs. inanimate—these categories are not used by young children at all.

The young child's world is seen very much, in fact almost exclusively, from the child's own point of view. If you show a domino to a small child, black on one side with white dots on the other side, and then hold it so the white dots are facing the young child, the following will almost always happen:

"Can you see the dots?"

"Yes."

"Are there many or just one?"

"There are a whole bunch."

"Can I see the dots?"

"Yes."

"No. See, the black side is facing me," you say as you show the child your side of the domino. Then turning the domino back again so that the dots are again facing the child, you ask a second time, "Can I see the dots?"

"Yes."

Getting a little exasperated, you may try turning the domino over and showing the child the black side. "Now," you continue, "you see the black side, and I see the dots, right?"

"Right."

"Now, can I see the black side?"

"Yes."

By this time most adults will decide that this is a stupid kid and give up in frustration.

But little children are not stupid. They merely see the world exclusively from their point of view; they are egocentric. Piaget discovered the fact that little children are egocentric. He also discovered that they do not distinguish between inside and outside.

Everyone gets upset when something that they care about gets broken, but a little child may be devastated by a broken toy or cookie.

"Oh, Mommy," Johnny wailed, "I can't eat this one!" as he held up a cookie with the corner broken off.

"Why not?" his mother asked.

"It's apart. It's broken."

"But you always take the top off and eat the icing first."

"No. It's no good. It's broken," Johnny protests, becoming increasingly hysterical.

Two-year-old Johnny is not just being "terrible" or stubborn. To a two-year-old a beloved thing outside is like a broken part inside. The hysteria over the broken cookie ought to be compared to the hysteria we would feel if the doctor told us we had a defective part of our body. Young children do not really believe that their bodies stop at their finger-

tips. Their bodies include everything that they feel attached to.

"Don't step on my shadow. You'll hurt me!" little Sara cries in panic. She has not yet understood that her shadow is not a part of her.

There are many other things that Piaget discovered besides children's egocentricity and their tendency to think that inside the body and outside the body are the same, but these ideas will give you a sense of the way a small child looks at the world.

I've spent this time on Piaget because Charlotte Ellinwood started her study of how a child talks about feelings with Piaget. She felt that his insights into the thinking of a child would be helpful in uncovering how a child feels and, more importantly, how they understand how they feel. And she was right.

Let me begin to share some of Charlotte Ellinwood's insights with you.

First, Dr. Ellinwood predicted, and the data that she collected supported the idea, that a child would only very gradually learn to use feeling words and that initially the feelings would be seen as belonging to the object rather than to the subject.

Very young children, up to about two years of age, rarely use feeling words at all. They can let you know what they want: "out," "up," or "cookie." They let you know by facial expressions and vocal sounds how they feel. But they hardly ever tell you in words how they feel.

Later on, during the preschool years, children begin to use feeling words, but instead of the feelings being seen as inside the child, the feelings are viewed as being in the object:

"That's a yucky picture." (Instead of, "I don't like it.")

"You're a bad daddy." (Instead of, "I'm angry at you.")

"Bad sidewalk!" (Instead of, "I tripped and hurt my knee.")

As the child goes through elementary school, feelings become owned as one's own, but the focus is on the outside.

"I don't like that picture."

"That made me angry." (Instead of, "I feel angry.")

Still later, usually not before early adolescence, the child begins to focus on the subjective side of the feeling. They have the feeling as an inner experience. Frequently, a form of the verb *to be* is used.

"I'm angry."

"I feel so happy I could pop!"

Not until mid-adolescence, or even later, do children become capable of completely separating inner and outer, subject and object, with a resulting ability to elaborate on what they are feeling.

"My insides feel like a teapot that's almost ready to whistle."

"I'm so happy it feels like tiny crystal bells are tinkling in my head."

The differentiation between inner and outer, subjective and objective, is only one dimension of the change that occurs in children's ability to understand and talk about feelings. There is another, second dimension that changes as the child gets older. This is the dimension of expression of the feeling.

When young children, who don't distinguish between inner and outer, *express* feelings, they express them in simple, unelaborated ways:

"Yeah!"

"Ow."

"Ugh."

"Yippee!"

A preschool child, on the other hand, is capable of *describing* a feeling rather than only expressing it:

"Mommy sad?" while looking at Mommy's tear-stained cheeks.

"My finger hurts."

As children continue into elementary school, they begin to develop an ability to elaborate on the feeling they are expressing or describing. They also begin to recognize causation:

"Is mommy sad because everything burned?"

"I cut my finger on the glass. It hurts."

As the child enters adolescence, the expression and description of feelings (their own and other people's) get increasingly elaborate:

"Mom, I know the dinner burned, but it's not so bad. We can always go out to McDonald's.

"I wish I had been more careful. I cut my finger on the piece of glass I was trying to pick up. It sure does sting."

Finally, during later adolescence, children become capable of *exploring* their feelings, not only in terms of causation, but also in terms of the feeling's meaning:

"Mom, how come you're so upset? Dinner's gotten burned before. Is it because tonight is Dad's birthday?"

"I guess I'm more angry than hurt. I shouldn't have dropped the glass in the first place, and I certainly should've picked it up more carefully."

Charlotte Ellinwood discovered several other things about the changes that occur in a child's ability to talk about feelings, but these two dimensions will give us enough to work with. Basically, what she found was that as children become older, they become increasingly capable of talking about their feelings. They separate inner and outer reality. They are able to express, describe and explore their feelings. But these abilities develop very slowly —which brings us not only to the point of this chapter, but to the point of the book.

WHAT DO WE DO WITH
ALL THESE FACTS?

As adults who care about children, we want them to be able to talk about their feelings and be able to express their feelings in clear, nondestructive ways. The problem is that most of what we have heard about how to help children with their feelings has not taken into consideration the *ability* of children to do that.

We wouldn't think of asking a child who couldn't

count to try to solve a problem in algebra, yet every day I see parents trying to get preschool children to talk about their feelings.

"Now tell me what's wrong. Why are you crying?" A very reasonable question to address to a school-age child or even a bright preschooler, but if you expect your toddler to tell you, you're in trouble.

In the next four chapters we will look in greater detail at what we can expect from children at different ages regarding the expression of feelings: the young child, the school-age child, the adolescent, and the young adult. From time to time I will add other insights from Dr. Ellinwood, but mostly I want to give more examples of what we've already discussed.

Don't be discouraged if you have not quite caught on to what Dr. Ellinwood is suggesting about children and their feelings. I said her ideas were simple, but I didn't say they were easy.

4

The Young Child and the Expression of Feelings

"Daddy!" Robbie cries excitedly as he comes racing around the corner and leaps into my arms.

Robbie is three and a half, and we have been performing this ritual for over a year now. I say "ritual" because it is a ritual, with rules and regulations that must be carefully observed.

Robbie has to start from the door of the den, which is at the opposite end of the living room from the front door. He has to run the length of the living room at full speed. I have to remain waiting in the hall until he leaps into my arms, and then he has to be lifted high over my head so that he nearly touches the ceiling. As I lift him, I have to call out his name, "Robbie!"

Any diversion destroys the ritual. If he should happen to be in the hall as I arrive home from work, and if I should try to pick him up to give him a kiss, the results are catastrophic.

"No! No! Put me down!" he will scream, followed by a distraught display as he lies on his face on the hall rug.

Any deviation can cause the same reversal of affect, from complete joy to complete desolation. An older brother or sister who impedes his progress as he runs through the living room, my failure to lift him the full length of my arms over my head —these changes are not, cannot be, tolerated.

AN EMOTIONAL CYCLONE

Robbie at three and a half is given to rapid, dramatic shifts of affect, and so were our other three children when they were young. In fact, rapid shifts of feeling or affect are one of the characteristics of the young child's expression of feeling.

Some parents, particularly young parents, find these swings unnerving: "We were sitting together reading a book. He seemed so content on my lap, and suddenly he slid to the floor sobbing." Or, "One minute she loves me and the next minute she hates me. What's wrong with my child?"

Probably nothing. At least not if your child is a preschooler. Rapid, dramatic shifts in feeling are simply a part of what it means to be a young child.

"If it's normal and necessary, I suppose I have to put up with it, but in the meantime how do I handle it?" you might well ask.

Before I answer your question, allow me to di-

gress a bit. There is some additional background that would be helpful before I make any specific suggestions about how to survive your "emotional cyclone."

INTO YOUR OWN PAST

I'd like you to think back as far as you can into your own past, to an event that comes from your own preschool years. It may be a vivid memory or a vague one. It may be like a snapshot or a short film. Remember in as much detail as you can— what you saw, touched, tasted, thought, ·felt like. Just stop reading for a few minutes and remember.

In case you're having difficulty, let me share one or two memories out of my own history.

The first memory comes from a time when I was about two years of age. The memory is like an old film clip. The light is bad, and the whole memory lasts only a few seconds.

Down the hill from the house where I spent the first two and one-half years of my life was the Baltimore harbor. Near it were train tracks that were used to load and unload the great ships. Sometimes in the evening my father would take my older brother and me down to the railroad tracks. One evening—at least I suspect it was evening from the dim light of my memory—my father lifted me up into an empty boxcar.

Since both doors were open, I could see out the other side of the car, and for a moment I felt like a giant—powerful, tall—and then I started to feel afraid, so my father lifted me back down to the ground.

That's the whole memory: up into the boxcar, feelings of power followed by fear, and back to "safety" again.

Or a second memory. A little later in my life, when I was almost three, we had moved to a new house, north of the harbor. I was standing at the bottom of a hill. Ahead of me was a sidewalk lined with hedges higher than my head. I held a rag doll in my right hand. As the doll hung limply on the ground beside me, I tried to decide whether or not to go up the hill. The same mixture of fear and excitement were present as in the boxcar, for this too was a *first time*, a new experience.

As adults, one of the things that we tend to forget is that a young child has many, many new experiences each day. The infant discovering his hand, the toddler finding that she can walk, the preschooler exploring the world outside the home—incidents that in our forgetfulness we often take for granted—are new, delightful, but also terrifying for the young child.

EVERYTHING'S NEW

The young child's experiential history is so short that newness is commonplace. New food, new feelings, new sights and sounds—the infant and young child are surrounded by novelty.

If you add to their lack of experience an immature nervous system, you begin to understand why small children's feelings change so much. Constancy is a rarity for a young child. It is something they need and treasure, yet seldom have for very long, because things are always changing for them, changing in a way that may be imperceptible to us adults who have had our senses dulled by time and repetition, but very noticeable to the young child, sometimes distressingly so.

We adults sometimes find ourselves thinking, "I wish things wouldn't change so much," but the feeling that accompanies such a thought is likely to be a bittersweet nostalgia. For a young child change, particularly rapid or dramatic change, is overwhelming, because it threatens their fragile security, their as yet only partially developed sense of continuity within the change they experience so constantly.

So, when you start to think about how to handle your constantly changing preschooler's feelings, remember for a moment that to them the world is changing much faster than it seems to be to you, so fast that at times they get overwhelmed. Put yourself in their place for a moment before you decide or even think about how to handle their lack of emotional constancy.

Imagine yourself in a foreign country, everything new and strange; or speed time up by ten and multiply your sensory acuity by the same factor, and then you will begin to get a feel for what the experience of a young child is like.

When you get a feel for what it is like to be a young child, then their dramatic shifts of affect make more sense. In fact, their rapid changes of affect are the only sensible way to react to situations that seem so changeable and overwhelming.

WHAT DO I DO WITH A
YOUNG CHILD'S FEELINGS?

We still have left hanging the original question: how do you handle the shifting moods and feelings of a young child? The question may seem more understandable when we remember the young child's experience of the world, but, regardless of what causes the changes, *we* still have to do something with this changing unpredictable bundle of energy.

There are two ways to handle the rapidly shifting experiences of affect of young children—an oversimplification I recognize, but nevertheless true—my way and my wife's way. My wife's way is the correct way. So to get the bad example out of the way, let me first tell you how I usually handle a rapid mood change, particularly a change from very positive to very negative.

Let's go back to Robbie, charging across the living room floor. Just as he nears the hall, the dog trots out from the kitchen and Robbie comes to a stop to avoid falling over him. Since Robbie has stopped less than two feet away, I reach down, thinking that certainly the few inches will not mar our homecoming, and pick him up. Robbie turns into a wiggling mass of muscle and bone and demands to be placed on the floor.

"Robbie, this is ridiculous," I say with the full indignation of my superior intellect. "Why can't I lean over and pick you up instead of your jumping into my arms?" Of course my rational explanation serves to make him scream more loudly, and I retreat to the kitchen with a mumbled, "That boy!"

My way, the wrong way to react to a rapid change of affect in a young child, is to think that a rational explanation will solve it. Not only will a rational explanation fail to dissolve the problem, it is almost guaranteed to make it worse.

What I should do is to get inside his world and see what has happened from his perspective. My wife usually does that. She has an uncanny ability to see things from a child's point of view. I, on the other hand, am seldom able to do so. I find it difficult to lay aside my 40 years of experience and many inches of height to get back to the perspective of a child. My wife seems to do it quite naturally. If I could become my wife Barbara for a moment, I might say to Robbie:

"That Scottie dog! He got in the way just at the wrong time. I know that makes you mad. Why don't you go back and run again. I'll wait here."

Robbie would stop his sobbing, slowly get up and walk back to the den. He would reappear around the corner, magically transformed into the same excited child I had seen when I first entered the house. The false start would be forgotten, and the ritual would be completed with the gleeful, "Daddy!" "Robbie!"

I see that my wife's way, taking the child's perspective and speaking out of his experience and feelings, works. It works beautifully for her, but it hardly ever works for me. Not primarily because I try it and it doesn't work, but because I almost always forget to try it until it's too late.

Some people have a knack for getting into the world of a small child. They seem to understand that world from the inside. Unfortunately I can count on one hand the people who have that ability to a high degree. My wife Barbara is one of them, and Charlotte Ellinwood is another. If, like myself, you happen not to be so blessed, what is to be done? How are you and I to handle our emotionally changeable preschoolers?

You might, with mechanical precision, feed back what you think your distraught three-year-old might be feeling. If you do, sometimes you will be right. You'll know when you are right because you will see a nearly magical transformation in your child.

Most of the time—if your average is anything like mine—you will miss. You will know you have missed because the screaming mass in front of you will continue to scream.

In my experience the best second step is to admit defeat and retreat. If you stay and make a second or third attempt at putting your child's feelings into words, you will probably have about the same success that one would experience in trying to put out a fire with wood alcohol. Please—for the sake of your child and your own nerves—retreat. After

the smoke has cleared, you can negotiate a settlement. To try to do so in the thick of the conflagration is foolhardy.

Fortunately, the rapidly changing affect of a young child has its compensations. Their black moods seldom last very long. A thundershower would probably be the best analogy for the young child's emotional storms.

I would suggest that you try to put your preschooler's feelings, or more precisely, what you think your preschooler's feelings are, into words. When you do it successfully, it is a delightfully satisfying experience for you and your child. But don't be too chagrined if your efforts fail, because children are very forgiving of our bungling attempts at helping them.

As we move toward the school years, the "storms" get milder but longer-lived. The "fair weather" also lasts for more extended periods. We shift our attention now to the older, school-age child, one with whom we can reason, one who makes us a little more comfortable because we feel ourselves more in the presence of a kindred spirit. We feel more at home with school-age children not only because their emotions are more stable than preschoolers', but also because they can *describe* how they feel rather than simply *express* it.

5

The School-Age Child and the Description of Feelings

I was eight, and my brother Don was five. We had gone with a group of people to Herring Run Park, hundreds of acres of woodland and grassy hills marred only by a polluted stream that ran along its western perimeter.

"You can play any place in the park you want, but stay away from the stream. It's polluted," our parents had told us. So of course we went immediately to the stream.

"Typhoid fever," they had said. "That's what you can catch if you go into the water."

Not knowing what typhoid fever was, we kept a respectful distance from the shallow, dancing brook, but fascinated by its destructive power, we were drawn to it as well. Its ability to destroy, hidden within the apparent clarity of its waters, was too intriguing to ignore.

As we walked along the east side of the stream, we heard a voice call to us from the other bank, "Stop! Stand still!"

We looked across the stream and up the fifty-foot embankment. At first we saw no one. We continued to walk.

"Stop, I said!" the voice cried again, and this time we saw him, a boy of about ten standing beside a tree about halfway up the hill.

The stream was about twenty feet wide, too wide to jump, and since it was polluted, we felt sure it would act as a moat to protect us from this "baron" who obviously seemed to think he owned the land.

When we continued walking south along the stream, the boy on the other side ran down the hill. He ran ahead of us on his side of the stream, and then about fifty yards ahead of us, he crossed to our side. At the same time four other boys emerged from the bushes near where we had been standing and crossed the stream behind us.

The boy ahead of us was slightly smaller than I, and since there was only one of him, we ran toward him. He seemed to have a stick in his hand. As we closed the distance, I said out loud to myself, "It's only a small stick."

When we got up to him, thinking that we could bump against him and rush on by, we were brought to a sudden stop by the recognition that the "small stick" was in fact a rusty knife with a 10-12″ blade.

This time when he commanded us to stop, we stopped.

The five boys led us back across the stream, polluted water oozing into our shoes, and up the hill to a cave that had been hidden by the underbrush.

"We live here," the boy with the knife said. And to prove his point he showed us several opened cans of beans and a half-eaten loaf of bread. I doubted his word, but decided that this was not a good time to get into a discussion about fantasy and reality.

He told us to sit down in the cave. We sat.

"We're going to keep you here with us," he said menacingly.

The thought of a night in the dark cave sent a chill up my back, but I said nothing.

"Watch this!" he said with great drama. "I'll show you what I can do with a knife." Three times he tried to stick the knife into a large oak tree about ten feet in front of us, and three times the knife fell to the ground.

Despite my fear I almost laughed as the knife hit the ground for the third time. Obviously embarrassed by his failure to impress us, the boy with the knife turned to me and said, "OK, we'll let you go, but first you'll have to knife fight me."

I had never been in a knife fight in my life, but our captor's face, with a particularly ugly scar that ran from his left eye to his upper lip, suggested that perhaps he had.

"I don't have a knife," I replied hopefully.

"Give him one," the boy with the knife said to one of his confederates.

As the boy attempted to get me to take his knife, I refused it. "No, I won't knife fight you," I said with a determination that was fueled by terror.

Several seconds passed as the boys looked at one another, then came a final alternative. "We'll let you go if you wrestle me," the leader said.

Finally, I felt on familiar ground. I had often wrestled with boys my age and older and knew that I could hold my own with anyone my size. This boy was slightly smaller than I. Further, and more important, wrestling holds might hurt, but they don't maim or kill.

"OK," I said quickly, "I'll wrestle you."

"Stand over there," he commanded as he climbed up on a stump. "I'll tell you when to start."

"Start!" he hollered, as he jumped from the stump onto my back.

To his surprise and mine, I quickly threw him over and got him down.

"Hold it, hold it!" he shouted. "We have to start over again." We started over again with me on the ground and him on top of me.

By now my younger brother had endured all he could, and he began to cry. It was only many years later that I realized that his sign of "weakness" was the correct strategy. I was so intent on winning the wrestling match that I probably would have escalated the fight back up to a deadly level. But my brother's tears saved us. We had "given in," and so we could be spared.

As I have looked back on that incident from the wisdom of over thirty years, I have been continually impressed by my determination and stupidity. I would not crack, I would not give up, and my "bravery" nearly cost me my life.

My younger brother, on the other hand, was still young enough to not have learned that it's not all right for boys to be afraid and even to cry. Fortunately for us both, he had been young enough to have been able to express his fear.

School-age children learn many things about their feelings, but mostly they learn not to express them.

REPRESSING FEELINGS

"Big boys don't cry."

"Don't get so excited!"

"Quit acting like a baby."

Even without these injunctions from older children and adults, an interesting phenomenon usually occurs during the early school years. From their exuberant expression in early childhood, feelings moderate and at times almost seem to vanish. The highly emotional two- and three-year-old becomes an almost placid eight- and nine-year-old. Why?

Reinforcement? Yes, that's part of the answer. We do encourage school-age children to be less expressive of their feelings.

But even when we do the opposite, even when we encourage our school-age children to "get their feelings out," the school-age child seems to have a built-in reticence to express feelings, particularly strong ones.

As the preschool child's affective expression is marked by unexpected storms, so the school-age child's affective expression is marked by a strange calm. The feelings that were too readily available before five are frustratingly absent after seven or eight.

But they are not gone, anymore than a sky without clouds has no water vapor in it. The feelings are still present, invisibly present perhaps, but not gone.

Where are they then? Sometimes underground in the unconscious, but sometimes just below the surface, felt by the child, but not expressed.

For the parent, the reprieve from emotional bombardment usually comes as a welcome respite. But what function does this calm serve for the child?

NEW SKILLS

The period from five or six years of age through later childhood is a time of rapid integration and development of a number of skills. Not only the more obvious skills of reading, writing, and arithmetic develop between the ages of six and twelve, but also physical and emotional skills.

In order for a child to move to the next level of emotional development — the ability to describe feelings rather than simply express them—the child needs to develop some distance from those feelings. You cannot describe something that you are completely involved with.

Have you ever had a very intense emotional experience and then tried to recall what happened? It's very difficult, not because you've repressed the memory, but because you were so caught up in what was happening that there was nothing of you left over to watch what was going on. There was no observing ego.

During the early school years children are not only trying to master academic and physical skills; they are also trying to gain some control over their own emotions. The distancing, or squashing of their emotions, is a first and necessary step in that process of achieving emotional control.

So if your eight-year-old doesn't seem to feel things the way she used to, don't fret over her loss of sensitivity. It'll be back. When it does return, it will be with a new maturity, for it will return with a sense of its being *in*, rather than *out of*, your child's control.

The sign that a school-age child is beginning to move into a new level of emotional maturity is her ability to describe her feelings. And that ability to describe how one feels must be preceded by the child's ability to become somewhat distant from the feeling to be described.

Initially the ability to describe a feeling will be simple and straightforward, but as the child matures, the descriptions will become quite elaborate. For example, the child just entering the descriptive level of affective development might say, "I'm angry," or "I'm scared."

This simple ability to *describe* a feeling is a major improvement over the younger child's reliance on

the *expression* of feeling, which would look more like, "You bad person!" or "Oooh! That's a scary face."

The older school-age child also recognizes that a feeling is something in her rather than an aspect of the object: "I'm angry," rather than, "You're bad."

Older school-age children have begun to separate subject and object enough so that they come to recognize that feelings are inside them, not inside the object. In a child's ability to handle feelings, the owning of a feeling as a function of describing it is one of the major changes that occurs during the school years.

Another advancement that begins toward the end of the preschool years and gets solidified during the school-age period is the ability to recognize that other people have feelings, too. "She's angry" or "She's scared" joins the feelings that a child recognizes in themselves. Being able to describe the feelings of others allows a child to take the role of the other person, which in turn is an important step in social and moral development.

Finally, in addition to the ability to describe one's own feelings and those of others, the school-age child also begins to recognize that feelings can be described in the past, present, or future.

The young child's feelings exist only in the present or the immediate past. Older preschool children or school-age children can talk about how they felt some days ago or even project themselves into the future and predict how they will feel then. "Tomorrow's my birthday. We're going to have a party. It's going to be fun." Or, "Last week I was mad at him."

This increasing ability to see the world as a continuing place and the self as having a past, present, and future is a skill that is not confined to affective development, but it does serve to help the school-age child become less reactive to the immediate environment. Change, rather than being at times the overwhelming experience that it is for the young child, is at least tolerated and even, during periods of strength, welcomed by the school-age child. In fact, too much of the same thing may result in boredom rather than security for an older child.

HOW ADULTS CAN HELP

As parents, teachers, adults who care about children, how can we use our knowledge of the school-age children's affective development to help them better understand their feelings? With preschool children it was suggested that we try to put a child's feelings into words, and there is no reason to stop doing so when a child reaches school. The only difference will be that we will be right more often, and even when we are wrong, sometimes an attempt at describing a feeling will help our child get rolling.

"Johnny, you're very quiet. Are you angry because I wouldn't let you play with Tony?"

"No, I'm not angry. I'm scared that Tony won't like me any more."

Such an ability to begin to compare feelings such as anger and fear, usually marks the end of the descriptive level of affective development. Toward the end of the school age period two other affective skills begin to appear:

1. The ability to compare feelings
2. The ability to explain feelings

These two skills signal the advent of adolescent emotional abilities, and it is to this fascinating period of development that we now turn our attention.

6

Adolescents and the Explanation of Feelings

Adolescence is frequently marked by the re-emergence of the rapid emotional changes of early childhood. Tears, laughter, silliness follow one another in rapid, at times dizzying, succession. Fortunately, for the adolescent and for those whose lives they touch, there is one big difference between a young child and an adolescent: adolescents can talk about their feelings.

Of all the feelings that an adolescent experiences and wants to express, the most powerful and most delightful feeling is that of love. In the following chapter we will be looking at adolescents' ability to talk about their feelings, using "falling in love" as the primary example.

REMEMBER WHEN

To start our exploration of the feelings of an adolescent, I will ask you once again to call on your own memories. Do you remember falling in love for the first time? Do you remember how old you were? How you felt?

I remember vividly. I was 15 and had been dating a girl named Joan for several months. I liked her, enjoyed being with her, but I was not in love with her.

Then one evening I joined her on a baby-sitting job. She had taken care of the infant before. The child's parents knew and trusted Joan. So when she asked if it would be OK if I joined her, they gave their approval.

We had been watching a movie on TV for about an hour when the baby cried. Joan got up from the sofa and went upstairs to the baby's room.

She had been gone for several minutes when a commercial came on. I went upstairs to see how she was doing with the baby. The baby's room was dark except for a night-light, but the hall was brightly lit. As I came to the top of the stairs, I saw Joan standing in the doorway with the baby's head nestled against her cheek. And I fell in love.

Something inside my chest ached, and I wanted to be with her forever. I didn't understand my feelings. I shared them with no one, including Joan, but I knew that I was *in love*.

The relationship ended up not working out, but I have not forgotten her or the feeling I had for her.

I suspect that most of you could tell similar stories of the first awakening of love, that strange combination of sexual lust, dependency, empathy, and comfort that signals the advent of adulthood.

Since being in love and talking about being in love are two of the primary activities of adolescence, it is appropriate that we should focus our attention there as we continue to try to understand how children think about and talk about their feelings.

The next major step that occurs in the ability of a growing person to master their feelings is that they add to the already existing abilities of *expressing* and *describing* their feelings, the ability to *explain* and *compare* feelings.

I LOVE YOU

If you were to ask a young child what he meant when he said, "I love you," you would in all probability get a blank stare. If you asked the same question of an adolescent, you may get very little response beyond an embarrassed silence, but the response would not fail to come because the adolescent really did not know how to respond, but rather because he did not want to.

If you could get inside the mind of that adolescent as a close peer is sometimes able to do, you would probably hear the following internal monologue:

"What does it mean 'I love you'? Well, I'm not sure exactly. I know I want to be with you, all the time. I feel good when we're together, and I miss you when we're apart. When I know I'm going to see you soon, my heart starts to beat faster and I feel excited. When I think about the future, you're always a part of my plans. I guess all of that's what I mean when I say 'I love you.' "

To this internal monologue suppose we were to add the second party, the person to whom these words ought to be expressed. And suppose further that we could unobtrusively overhear the conversation.

"Oh sure, you love me. How many other people have you said that to?"

"Nobody else."

"What about Mary Jane. Didn't you tell her you loved her?"

"Yeah, but that's not the same."

"What do you mean, it's not the same? You used the same words, didn't you?"

"Sure, but Mary Jane's like a sister to me. When I told her I loved her, it was the way I'd say it to a sister."

"Am I like a sister too?"

"No, not at all."

"What's different, then?"

"Oh, I'm not sure I can explain it."

"Well, you'd better try," her voice rising.

"Wait a minute, don't get excited. There's a difference, a big difference between the way I feel about you and the way I feel about Mary Jane. Just let me explain."

(A brief silence.)

"Well?"

"Just a minute. Did you ever kiss your brother?"

"Yes. What's that have to do with you and Mary Jane?"

"How did you kiss him?"

"Like this," pursing her lips.

"No. That's not what I mean. Where did you kiss him?"

"On the cheek."

"And what were you doing while you kissed him?"

"I was just standing there."

"Is that how I kiss you?"

"No."

"Where do I kiss you?"

"Oh, come on, this is getting silly."

"No, I mean it. Where do I kiss you?"

"In the hall, in the car."

"Come on, I'm serious."

"You kiss me on the lips."

"And am I standing with my arms at my sides?"

"Of course not. You're holding me."

"Do you understand the difference?"

"I understand the difference between kissing boyfriends and brothers, but what about Mary Jane?"

"If I'd kissed Mary Jane, and I haven't, I'd kiss her the way you do your brother. When I tell her, 'I love you,' it'd be the same way you'd tell your brother you love him."

"Are you *sure* that's the way you feel about Mary Jane? Just a sister, nothing more?"

"I'm sure. You're the only one I'm in love with."

LOVE AND BEING IN LOVE

A couple of five-year-olds couldn't have a conversation like the one above. Not only because five-year-olds don't usually have boy and girl friends (although some of them do), but because five-year-olds simply are not capable of comparing two kinds of feelings, especially two as similar as loving and being in love.

A five-year-old could say, "I love you," or perhaps even, "I like you better than Tommy," but the subtlety of comparison involved in distinguishing between *loving* and *being in love* is simply beyond them.

On the other hand, a fifteen-year-old has little or no trouble making such a distinction. And as anyone who has been *in love* knows, the distinction between loving and being in love is critical indeed.

Explaining and comparing feelings are abilities that rarely appear with any real facility before adolescence. The cognitive tools of formal reasoning that are so necessary to the process of comparison are simply not in place yet during childhood. And coincidentally, the ability to explain and compare feelings, so critical to being in love, seems to make its appearance just about the time it's needed.

Of course the ability to explain feelings or to compare two or more feelings with one another is not restricted to varieties of loving, but the shades and qualities of love certainly provide teen-agers with the full range of "gymnastic equipment" on which to exercise their growing affective abilities.

To clarify this ability to explain and compare feelings further, suppose we take a look at a feeling that frequently accompanies being in love— jealousy.

JEALOUSY

The feeling of jealousy has to do with the commitment side of a being-in-love relationship. The reason people look down on jealousy as a feeling is that it is usually associated with ownership: "I'm jealous of my boyfriend, girlfriend, husband, or wife because they belong to me." Even moderately sophisticated adults or adolescents do not want to see themselves as owning another person. But the feeling of jealousy did not disappear with the end of a property notion of human relationships. Rather, ownership was replaced by commitment. We no longer say that we own another person, but we do look for, expect, even demand a commitment from them in a love relationship.

Commitment is a mutual relationship between equals and therefore more closely describes the current ideal of an adult sexual relationship.

When the person we are in love with flirts with someone else or seems more interested in someone else than in us, we feel jealous. And so do adolescents.

To return to our hypothetical adolescent couple, let's see how they might talk about jealousy:

"As long as we're talking about other people, what about Tommy?"

"What about Tommy?"

"Mary Jane is like a sister to me, but I'm not so sure Tommy is like a brother to you."

"Oh, come on."

"No. Now don't just brush it off. Last Friday night at the roller rink when he asked you to skate during the couples' skate, you sure didn't waste any time saying 'yes.'"

"Tommy's a good skater, that's all."

"Oh. And what else is he good at?"

"I only skated with him one time. I went home with you, not him. What are you getting so upset about?"

"Watching the two of you skate around the rink almost made me crazy. I wanted to skate out onto the floor and pull his arm from around your waist. I wanted you back with me."

"Tommy doesn't mean anything to me. I can't see why you're jealous."

"Who said anything about jealousy? I just don't want the two of you skating together again, that's all."

"If you're not jealous, then why is it OK for me to skate with your brother, or my dad, or any of my girlfriends? Answer me that!"

"Well, I guess you do have a point. But it's not just the fact that the two of you skated together. It was the way you were skating — so close, so smooth, like you belonged together."

"Believe me. I like to skate with Tommy. He's good, the best skater I know, but you're my boyfriend."

"It's just that you mean so much to me."
"And you know how I feel about you."

PRIVACY

As adults, what can we do to help adolescents toward affective maturity? Are there some things that as parents or concerned adults we can do to help them not only express their feelings but also to understand those feelings?

Perhaps the best thing we can do for adolescents is to give them some privacy. One of the reasons that adolescents, particularly younger adolescents, spend so much time on the phone is that the phone gives them a safe, private way to communicate feelings. The person at the other end of the line can hang up on you, but he can't kill you or kiss you. Moreover, a phone call provides a fairly private opportunity to communicate.

As an adolescent I can remember that I always asked a girl for a date by phone. I didn't want to see how she looked, or let her see how I looked while I was asking. And I especially didn't want anyone else to overhear our conversation, particularly if it resulted in my being turned down.

I know those hours on the phone can be aggravating for the rest of the family, but they do provide an outstanding vehicle for affective expression.

INDEPENDENCE

In addition to giving adolescents privacy, the other thing we can do for them, particularly if

they are our own children, is to allow them opportunities to talk to people other than us. I know parents and adolescents are supposed to communicate with one another. In fact, parent-child communication is supposed to be the key to raising emotionally healthy children. But the fact is that most adolescents would rather talk to anybody but their parents.

Certainly there are times when parents and adolescent children need to talk with one another. Family schedules need to be worked out. Conflicts need to be resolved. But when it comes to ordinary, everyday figuring-things-out kind of conversation, that should be not between child and parent but between child and almost anyone else.

It might be well to remind ourselves at this point that one of the major tasks of adolescence, at least in our society, is to gain independence from one's parents.

The sharing of feelings, particularly highly charged ones, is the surest way to create closeness. The closeness is not always comfortable. It may be the closeness of two "prize fighters," but strong emotions are sure to create interpersonal closeness.

Adolescents, on the other hand, are not trying to create closeness with their parents; they're trying to create distance. They don't need to get more in touch; they need to have more distance.

So when your adolescents seem to share less and less of themselves with you, don't get too upset. What they're doing is necessary, and not all that different from what they did with their own feelings as younger children.

Remember how young children need to get away from their feelings so they can gain some mastery over and understanding of those feelings? Much the same kind of thing needs to happen between adolescents and their parents. They need to create some distance so that they can understand you and their relationship with you. They'll be back to you as surely as they came back to their own feelings. But when they come back, it will be with a greater sense of ease and comfort both for them and you.

A SPECIAL NOTE FOR STEP-PARENTS

One reason that it's so difficult to add a step-parent to a family with one or more adolescents is that two conflicting demands are being expressed:

1. On the one hand, step-parents want to establish a relationship of closeness and trust. In fact, they need to if they are going to serve as parents.

2. At the same time, adolescents are moving away from parents, and the overtures of closeness are likely to be rebuffed because they are trying to create some emotional space for themselves.

About the only thing that can be done with this dilemma is to recognize it, spell it out for everyone involved, and then try to move toward a compromise of closeness—distance that is fairly satisfactory for everyone involved. It's not an easy task, so don't get discouraged. But it's also not impossible if parent, step-parent, and children are all willing to try to make it work.

ADOLESCENTS AND THEIR FEELINGS

Privacy and the opportunity to talk to other people about their feelings — these are the two major roles for the parents of adolescents.

Those of you who work with adolescents in non-parental or quasi-parental roles still need to respect adolescents' desire for privacy, but you may also find yourself being used as a "bridge" by some adolescents.

As an adolescent, I can remember using adult neighbors, Sunday school teachers, a variety of male and female adults to help me think through a range of emotionally charged crises.

One of the joys of teaching, coaching, or other work with youth is the opportunity to be helpful to someone who is not only trying to understand their feelings, but also the world and how they fit into it. They may talk to you about almost any feeling, and it is an honor that they trust you enough to use you to figure out something important.

Jealousy and being in love are only two of the hundreds of feelings that adolescents are capable of talking about with their peers or with nonparent adults. But one thing that most adolescents are not particularly good at is the ability to explore the feelings they have.

An adolescent, particularly a younger adolescent, can express a feeling, describe it, explain it, but explore it? No, that ability does not usually appear until young adulthood. It is to this final ability, the ability to explore a feeling, that we now turn our attention.

7

The Young Adult
and
Understanding Feelings

Young children express feelings; young adults
may understand them. I don't mean to suggest that
young adults no longer express feelings, that growing up means to stop expressing how you feel—not
at all. Young adults, in fact, are capable of expressing their feelings and expressing a wider, more
subtle range of feelings than young children. The
big difference between young children and young
adults is the young adult's ability to *understand*
his own and other people's feelings.

It must be obvious by now that the ability to
understand feelings does not simply blossom out
of bare ground. The ability to *understand* feelings
has grown out of the ability to *express* feelings, to
describe them, and to *explain* them. Only after this

whole "plant" has developed can the "flower" of understanding a feeling finally bloom.

I have worked as a psychotherapist for a number of years. In my work people come with a variety of problems—anxiety, depression, marital discord, problems with children or older parents. While I use a variety of techniques to assist them in finding a solution to their problems, one approach I use frequently is trying to help them to understand their feelings. I'd like to describe for you how I help people explore and understand their feelings.

TRYING TO GET OUT

At the beginning of the book it was suggested that a feeling was "something inside that needed to come out." That description of a feeling could also be applied to a variety of body functions, for example, breathing. Would you try an experiment with me?

Take a deep breath and hold it for ten seconds. Now try to hold it another ten seconds. Feel what is starting to happen? There is an increasing sense of pressure and urgency. It's as if the stale air in your lungs were trying to come out. (By the way, if you haven't exhaled by now, please do so!)

Feelings are much like that stale air in your lungs in that they need to come out. However, a feeling is more complex than the air in your lungs. In distinction to the stale air, it's not always clear how a feeling ought to come out, or what the feeling is that ought to come out. When you need to breathe out, there's not much question about how to do it; you simply stop holding your breath. The expression of a feeling, on the other hand, may involve a variety of facial expressions, words, or actions. That can make the correct expression of the feeling very complicated.

The advantage that young adults have over younger children is that they potentially have the ability to explore a feeling that is fighting to come out and then make a decision about *how*, or even *if*, they want to express it.

While the following example borders on being overly dramatic, I'd like to use it because it clearly demonstrates the process of understanding a feeling.

EXPLORING A FEELING WITH ACTIVE IMAGINATION

Kathy (not her real name) had come to therapy with a variety of symptoms: dizziness, depression, shortness of breath, inability to find an appropriate boyfriend, uncertainty about her career. She was 19 when she started therapy, and many of her concerns were typical of a person of her age. Her problem was that she was not getting closer to a solution to any of them. She had had one unsuccessful love affair after another. She went to college briefly, dropped out, tried a variety of jobs, had anxiety attacks, cried for no apparent reason. Nothing seemed to be working.

A mess, you say? Yes, but Kathy had one thing going for her: she could look at her feelings. She

had the ability to explore her feelings by engaging in internal fantasy. She could, in effect, dream with her eyes open. She could sit quietly in my office and describe the pictures that her unconscious mind produced. It was rather like going to a movie. Only neither Kathy nor I ever had the opportunity to read a "review" beforehand. In fact we seldom even knew the "title" of the "film." My job with Kathy was not to teach her how to explore her feelings using her fantasizing, but rather to help her to take her ability seriously. These fantasies of Kathy's were so vivid that it was as if she were living them rather than merely watching them. If she pictured a flower, she could tell me not only the size, shape, color, number of petals, but also what it smelled like and how it felt against her cheek. When Kathy pictured a scene, she was there.

One critical ingredient in the therapy was that Kathy learned that her inability to control the fantasies was not something to be feared. When she relaxed and let the fantasy take her wherever it "wanted" to go, she discovered that she frequently found out important, hidden things about herself.

As the months progressed, Kathy became increasingly adept at allowing herself to engage in vivid, uncontrolled fantasies during the therapy hour. During the particular session that I want to share with you, Kathy had started the session by describing to me a mountain that she was attempting to climb.

In her fantasy she was pressed against a mountain, attempting to find a place to get a firm grip, but she felt that she was slipping. The ground under her hands and feet had begun turning to mud, and she was frantically trying to maintain her position on the hill.

As she became increasingly frightened, I asked her what would happen if she were to let go. "I can't! I'll fall!" she replied.

"What will you fall into?" I asked.

"I don't know, but I can't let go!" she said with great agitation.

She continued to struggle silently for another five or ten minutes. Kathy was becoming increasingly anxious and exhausted until she was about to collapse. "I can't hold on anymore," she sobbed, as her body went limp.

Almost instantly her sobs turned into laughter. "What is it?" I asked, as her laughter became louder and more joyful.

"My waters aren't polluted. My waters aren't polluted!" she exclaimed. "I fell back and there was clear, pure water at the bottom of the mountain—not the awfulness I feared, but clear, pure water."

After that session Kathy began to make rapid progress. She remembered a series of long repressed memories about her early childhood which had severely retarded her ability to develop emotionally. Kathy adopted the day of the session, July 31, as her new birthday.

Let me use another example. Bob (not his real name) had been in psychotherapy for several years. Like Kathy, he made use of vivid fantasies in the therapy hours. During one session he found himself in a cave. It was dark, damp, and barren. He was aware that his therapist was outside the cave. He turned toward the opening and saw his therapist standing at the entrance with her right hand extended, beckoning to him. He wanted to take her hand, but he was frightened.

He vacillated back and forth for what seemed like an extremely long time. Finally, with a great deal of anxiety, he took her hand. Immediately he was outside.

He was in a warm, sunny meadow. People were laughing and dancing in a huge circle. With tears of joy in his eyes he joined in the dance. This session marked the beginning of a period of rapid progress, including the uncovering of long repressed memories and experiences.

Both Kathy and Bob used their ability of active imagination to help them sort out some very complicated feelings, but active imagination is only one way to explore a feeling.

FEELING A FEELING

In addition to active imagination or fantasizing, one can sometimes look directly at the feeling itself, paying attention to both the bodily sensation and the thoughts that are associated with the feeling.

I'll give an example of the second way to explore a feeling in a moment, but first I want to remind you that most of the time, young adults do not use their ability to understand their feelings in ways that are as dramatic as Kathy and Bob, but they can. And the fact that they can explore their feelings usually makes a young adult a much better candidate than a child or adolescent for inward-looking psychotherapy.

In addition to using the ability to understand feelings to get things accomplished in psychotherapy, the young adult can use that same ability in a variety of ways. Not everyone explores their feelings through watching pictures in their heads. Some people do it by paying attention to their dreams. Others do it by attending to bodily sensations.

For example, some years ago I discovered that sometimes when I was upset, I would get a tight feeling in my stomach. Rather than ignoring the tight feeling, I found it was usually much more beneficial to pay attention to the tightness in my stomach and then relax my body as much as possible.

As I relaxed, ideas would pop into my head, ideas that were usually related to the tension in my stomach. I learned to use my tight stomach muscles as a kind of radar system. It warned me of things that I was doing, or not doing, that I ought to pay attention to. It also frequently helped me to locate a problem with someone in my environment—a friend, a patient, or a colleague.

TALKING TO YOURSELF

Some young adults demonstrate their ability to understand their feelings by being able to carry on an internal dialogue to explore a feeling. Let me suggest an example:

"I feel warm," a young woman thinks to herself as she carries a pizza to a couple in the corner of the restaurant.

"Is it hot in here?"

"Let me check. No, the thermostat is set on a comfortable temperature and the thermometer seems to be working."

"Well, what's wrong then?"

"I'm only 20. I doubt if I'm having hot flashes. My forehead doesn't feel warm; I don't think I have a fever."

"Well, what is going on then?"

"Maybe I ought to think about it symbolically: 'It's getting hot in here.'"

"What does that mean? Maybe 'on the hot seat' or 'trouble brewing'? Or both?"

"I think it's both. I've had an uneasy feeling that something's not quite right about this new job. There's too much money around for a pizza parlor. I hate to admit it to myself, but I think maybe the owner is dealing in drugs."

Hunches, intuitions, fantasies, bodily sensations —all of these are fuel for the young adult's emotional engine. Feelings can be used to figure out what is wrong within one's own psyche and within one's environment.

DREAMS, DREAMS, DREAMS

One final technique that can be used to explore a feeling is the dream. Dreams at night are much like the uncontrolled fantasies of Kathy and Bob. They are potentially filled with information about our feelings.

Several years ago I had a vivid dream in which I was standing behind myself looking at my own neck. In the back of my neck was a deep cancerous looking wound. I awoke very frightened, with the dream vividly embedded in my conscious mind.

I tried to figure out the meaning of the dream, but could make no headway. Finally I talked with a friend who is also a psychotherapist, and she suggested that perhaps my unconscious mind was suggesting that there was a "break" between my mind and my body. I had entered middle age and had begun to exercise less and weigh more. Perhaps, she suggested, I was telling myself that I needed to increase my daily exercise. I began riding my bike rather than driving for any trip under five miles and found that within a few months the slightly sore throats that used to signal fatigue had almost disappeared.

The dream had alerted me to a problem that was developing, and it gave me the opportunity to avoid more serious problems. At least it did when I finally uncovered the message.

Dreams are not always easy to interpret. Frequently telling them to another person will help you to see the message. At other times someone else may have to interpret the message for you. The only way to be sure that you've hit on the correct interpretation is to see if the interpretation works.

But regardless of how we explore them, feelings are not just indicators of problems; they can also be signs that things are going well. Our dreams, our bodily sensations, the pictures inside our heads can be messengers of good news as well as bad.

One such set of feelings that people used to pay a great deal of attention to, and probably all of us ought to pay more attention to, are religious feelings.

In the next chapter we will use religious feelings as the paradigm for the positive use of feelings. We have saved religious feelings for now, not because young children do not have them, but because true understanding of religious feelings demands of us a combination of the wisdom of old age and the openness of childhood.

8

Religious Feelings

People of all ages have religious feelings, but to understand our own religious feelings we need to be old and young, wise and open, at the same time.

While religious feelings do not wait until adulthood to find expression and during adolescence may be one of our most powerful feelings, it is nevertheless true that the range of feelings that we usually designate as "religious" do not usually appear until adulthood

Carl Jung, the Swiss psychologist, suggested that religion was one of the most important experiences of a person's life. He further suggested that the latter part of life, after 40 years of age, was for spiritual development.

SPIRITUAL DEVELOPMENT

As biological beings our lives really should be over at forty. By forty our children are raised, and if we use biological maturity as the appropriate age for our children to have children, then by the time we are forty, our children should be parents. Once our children have had children, there is no question of the survival of the species, so why don't we all just die at age forty? One answer given by Jung and others is that the second half of life is given to us not for biological, but for psychological and spiritual, reasons.

This idea is by no means unique to the Western mind; many individuals in the East devote (or at least used to devote) the latter half of their lives to meditation, contemplation, and the spiritual life. While few people in the West have the inclination or the opportunity to devote themselves completely to the spiritual life, the fact remains that religious feelings become increasingly cogent for many people as they reach adulthood.

RELIGIOUS FEELINGS

There is no single feeling that qualifies as *the* religious feeling. In fact, any feeling is capable of being used as part of a spiritual quest. Love, hate, fear, wonder, joy, sadness—all can be incorporated into a person's religious experience.

The one feeling that seems to be particularly, and perhaps exclusively, related to religious experience

is described by Rudolph Otto in *The Idea of the Holy*. That feeling is *awe* or *holy fear*.

Holy fear is not a common experience for modern Western man. In fact, we sometimes consider ourselves as too sophisticated for such a feeling. Holy fear might have been appropriate for Moses as he stood gazing at the burning bush, or the people of Israel as they gathered around Mount Sinai, but we feel far removed from such events. But are we?

What is that "spooky" feeling we get sometimes when we hear or see a particularly vivid account of an event in the history of Israel or the life of Christ? Why the goose bumps? Why the combination of attraction and fear? Is it possible that sophistication and education are not the opposite of that "primitive" holy fear? Is it possible that even the most enlightened among us may still be subject to these so-called primitive emotions?

As people who value religious history, religious education, theological thinking, biblical study, is it not at least a little strange that we should shy away from religious feelings? Are emotions not to be allowed into our religious lives?

Of course, we do let them in occasionally. What would Chrismas be without carols, or Easter without music? Since music is one of the most common ways of expressing affect, we certainly cannot say that our emotions are kept out of religion completely.

Yet do we not grow uncomfortable when someone seems "carried away" by religion? Does not the idea of the Spirit actively involved in the life of an individual or group make us uneasy?

It does, and it should, because, as the New Testament reminds us, not all spirits are from God. We are admonished to test the spirits to see if they are good or evil. While the best test of a spirit is the results it produces, there are times when we cannot wait to see if the spirit will produce love or discord, peace or hatred. There are times when we want to know a little earlier in the process: is this feeling that seems to be urging me to do something really from God or not?

ABRAHAM AND ISAAC

Imagine a modernized version of the thinking of Abraham when his son Isaac was to be offered as a sacrifice. Suppose we apply the expression of feeling levels that we have been describing to Abraham and his dilemma over the requested sacrifice of his son Isaac. Certainly the first level of affective development, the *expression* of feeling would be appropriate:

"God, what are you up to?" Abraham might well ask.

But obviously the mere expression of feeling would not take Abraham very far in figuring things out. He might then shift to the next level and try to *describe* what he is feeling as a means of getting a handle on whether or not to take seriously this horrible request that he kill his son: "I'm scared.

I'm scared I'm going to kill my son, and then I'll feel awful."

This is more enlightening than the simple expression of the feeling, but still not helpful in determining whether the voice is coming from God, the devil, or Abraham's own disturbed unconscious. Perhaps if we try the next level, with Abraham trying to *explain* his feelings to himself:

"Well, of course, you're scared, Abraham. You don't know if this voice is God's or your own. You don't know if you're about to do something magnificent or horrible. No wonder you're scared."

We've succeeded in getting a sense of Abraham's terrible discomfort, but we still haven't helped him to determine where the voice is coming from and what he should do in response to it. In order to get an answer to such an awful question we need to move to the final level of affective development, the level of *exploration*:

"I know I'm scared. In fact, I'm terrified. I've never been so scared in my life. I'm scared because . . . well, because there's no right answer. If I kill Isaac, and the voice is God's, I will have made the greatest sacrifice a man could make, his own son; but I will also have destroyed the basis for my covenant with God, since Isaac was to be the source of a great nation.

"If I kill Isaac, and the voice is not God's, I will have destroyed myself, I will have killed the son I love, and I will have broken the covenant with God because Isaac is to be the source of God's promise to make a great nation from me.

"If the voice is God's, and I do not kill him, I will have disobeyed God, and the *most* important relationship in my life, my relationship with God, will be destroyed.

"If the voice is not God's, and I do not kill Isaac, then I will have narrowly avoided a great tragedy.

"Which is it? Kill or not kill? God or not God? Maybe if I pay more attention to the feeling itself. My stomach is fluttering. My hands are wet from perspiration. My vision is slightly blurred. My heart is pounding. I feel like a bowstring that has been stretched too tight and then plucked. But there beneath the terror is a quiet place, a place in me that nods, 'Yes. Yes, go ahead. Don't be afraid.'

"Is that madness? No, I don't think so. Is it the devil? He is a trickster, but I don't think he has reached my inner core where this head nods yes. That place has always been reserved for God. The voice must be God's."

As he raises the hand that holds the knife: "I will strike. What stays my hand? I cannot bring it down."

"Abraham! Abraham!" a voice calls.

OUR OWN RELIGIOUS FEELINGS

Our own religious experiences rarely carry such awful messages or arouse such storms of feelings, but we still have periods of extreme discomfort and uncertainty in our relationship with God.

"Should I marry her or not? Is she the right person for me?"

"Am I really meant to be a pastor? Does the call come from God or from my desire to be different?"

"The gift is so large. Should I really give it? Is it love that compels me or a desire to be noticed?"

Add dilemmas of your own. For if you have become involved with God in more than a passing way, you have certainly had times when it has been unclear whether the "voice" that calls within you is his or your own.

While nothing gives absolute certainty in the face of a religious dilemma, the ability to explore your own feelings and carry on an internal dialogue about them is a useful tool in ferreting out the source and the truth of what might be a religious feeling.

Perhaps one more example, a personal one, would be helpful.

Sometime ago I went to visit in a congregation that I had not visited before. I knew that there had been a history of problems there, so when I entered the church, I was pleased to find that a congenial group was meeting for coffee and tea in a room off the sanctuary. While I did not sense that everything was completely "together" for this group of people, I was pleasantly surprised by the fairly warm, relaxed atmosphere of the gathering.

After coffee was over, we all moved into the sanctuary for the service. The first part of the service went smoothly. The congregation and choir sang with enthusiasm. The pastor seemed to be genuinely glad to welcome us, and he led us well in worship.

When the pastor got into the pulpit, however, everything changed. It was as though a dark cloud had spread from him over the entire congregation.

As I sat in the pew, it became increasingly difficult for me to remain still. It was not only that the sermon was somewhat disorganized or that there were a few phrases that apparently had meaning for the established members, but had no meaning for me as a visitor; rather my discomfort seemed to come from the preacher himself.

In order to give myself something to do while I waited for the sermon to end and also because I am by habit an introspective person, I began to carry on the following dialogue with myself:

"What is this discomfort about? Too much coffee at the coffee hour?"

"No, I don't think so. I had only one cup, and the other cup I had this morning was several hours ago. No, I don't think I can attribute this uneasy feeling to caffeine."

"Well, what is it then?"

"I think I'm responding to the preacher."

"Responding, how?"

"Well, I feel kind of jittery and slightly depressed. I feel like I want to get out of here, as though there were a noxious stimulation here, like something that smells bad or is too loud."

"Now wait a minute. Are you sure that you're not just projecting your own discomfort onto the preacher? You are here for the first time. You are a stranger. Are you sure that the discomfort you feel is not just anxiety about whether or not you'll be accepted?"

"Oh, that may be a small part of it. But this feeling doesn't feel like a fear of being rejected; it feels more like I've come in contact with someone who is depressed and angry."

"Now, don't squirm off the hook so easily. How do you know that you're not the one who is depressed and angry and that you're not projecting it onto this poor preacher?"

"Well, I'm sophisticated enough to know that projection is unconscious, out of my awareness, but I really don't think that I am projecting the feeling. It feels much more like I'm receiving it, picking it up, rather than sending it out myself. Besides, why should I feel it only while he's preaching?"

"You do have a point there. Why not wait and see what happens after the sermon is over."

After the sermon was over, the "cloud" lifted. I related my experience to the pastor later, and he responded with considerable feeling: "I thought I had that under control. I've had problems with preaching for years. Somehow it seems to bring out the worst in me, but I thought I had solved that several years ago."

I recognize that the feeling I've just described was not a peculiarly "religious" feeling. I did not feel awe. I felt discomfort. But the context in which the feeling arose was religious, a church. The result of that feeling was religious, a show of concern for a fellow Christian. And the outcome clearly had religious implications, at least for me, and I hope for the pastor.

I was not *certain* I was on the right track until I shared my strange experience with the pastor, and he confirmed my impression. However, I have learned over the years that my hunches are usually correct, and so even if he had denied having any idea why I might have reacted so strangely to his sermon, I would still not have automatically dismissed my hunch as inaccurate. It is helpful, however, when a feeling receives external support.

All of us, to one degree or another, are intuitive people. We are people who have hunches, or unexplained feelings. Some people pay more attention to those hunches than others. Some people check them out while others ignore them. I'd like to suggest that you do yourself—and perhaps God—the courtesy of paying attention to those strange messages that sometimes flash into your mind. Don't accept them uncritically, even if they seem to come with great power and internal validity. The New Testament encourages us to test the spirits and to judge messages by the fruit that they bear. But if you do not take these messages seriously enough to check them out, you are doing yourself a disservice.

SUMMARY

We have covered a great deal of territory together. We started with a young child's simple expression of feelings and have now ended with messages from "beyond ourselves." Besides testing religious messages, what other use is there for what we have learned?

1. We have learned that children at different ages have differing abilities to express their feelings and that we ought to be careful to gear our explanations and conversations to their level.

2. In a previous book, *How to Bring Up a Good Child,* I discussed how important it was to know where children are in their moral development in order to gear our discipline to their developmental level. Knowing where a child is in emotional development also helps us to keep our explanations about moral issues within the child's level of emotional understanding.

3. Helping our children to describe and discuss their feelings decreases the likelihood of emotional disorder. No one can immunize a child against emotional distress, but a child who can discuss and examine his own emotional reactions is much more likely to handle an emotional crisis than one who cannot.

4. Finally, I hope that as you have read through this book about children, you have also been thinking about yourself. All of us could stand to develop our ability to *express, describe, compare* and *explore* our feelings. While the development of our ability to talk about our feelings may go on primarily during childhood and adolescence, development does not stop with adulthood. It is in fact a lifelong endeavor.

In the last chapter, we will start again with the young child and attempt to plug in what we have learned about emotional development to a variety of situations. There are things that we as adults who care about children can do to stimulate emotional development. And there are things that we need to remind ourselves about regarding how to help children handle their feelings.

9

What Do We Do Now?

Young children are one with their feelings, while older children and adults are somewhat removed from their feelings.

Young children can only *express* their feelings, while older children and adults can *talk about* theirs.

Older children can *describe* their feelings, while adolescents and adults can *compare* their feelings and *explore* them.

How do we use these facts in helping children tell us how they feel?

OUR OWN FEELINGS

The first and most important way for us to use this information is to apply it to ourselves. As adults, it is to our benefit and our children's if we *explore, compare, describe,* and *express* our own feelings.

In the last chapter I suggested how someone caught in a religious dilemma might explore a feeling. That same ability, the exploration of feelings, can be used in any difficult situation.

It isn't necessary to wait for a difficult situation to use the technique of exploring feelings. In fact, it's most desirable to regularly monitor how you feel. I know that Christians are usually told, "Don't pay any attention to yourself. Live for others." But if you're not functioning well, you're not likely to be very helpful to anyone else. Further, the Bible also states that we are God's temple, the place where he lives. If God lives in us, then it seems only right that we keep the place in good repair.

Checking on how one feels is a highly individual thing. Some people check several times a day; others don't check for weeks at a time. The critical issue is that you attend to negative feelings. The positive feelings usually take care of themselves. It's the ignored negative ones that get us into trouble. For example, if you check to see how you are feeling over a period of time, do you find that you're angry a lot? If you do, it would probably help if you took a few minutes to explore these angry feelings. You might do it alone, or you could sit down with a trusted friend.

"I've been angry a lot these past several months. Oh, I'm not always angry. Sometimes I feel happy, content, sad, lots of other feelings, but there is underlying anger most of the time, and I don't like it.

I don't like seeing myself as an angry person. I don't like what it does to other people."

"Rather than just trying to push it away, why not look at it more closely? What does this angry feeling feel like?"

"My jaw and the muscles around my mouth feel tight. I can feel tension across my upper back and neck. If I get really upset, there's a sense of pressure in my head or chest."

"Can you feel that feeling now?"

"Yes."

"Pay attention to it then. Relax and just focus your attention on it. What happens?"

"Well, my fist started to clench, and my eyes got narrower."

"What else?"

"I feel like I'm getting ready for a fight."

"With whom?"

"Everybody."

"Who particularly?"

"My husband, my kids."

"What are you angry at them for?"

"Demands, more and more demands. Every time I turn around, somebody's asking for something. They're driving me batty."

"Are the demands unreasonable?"

"No. Things like 'I need some clean socks.' 'What time is dinner?' Wait a minute, it's not just *their* demands; the house makes demands too: 'I'm dirty; dust me,' or 'I'm peeling, paint me.' It seems to never let up."

"What do you feel like doing about it?"

"Telling them all to drop dead!"

"And then?"

"Well, I don't really want them to be gone, but I do want, in fact, I *need* a break."

"Do you deserve one?"

"Of course I do. I work hard. In fact, I work too hard."

"How hard do the rest of them work—your husband, your children?"

"Oh, pretty hard I guess."

"As hard as you do?"

"I'm not sure. My husband works outside the home. He's tired when he gets home. The kids are in school all day. They need a break when they come home."

"And you? When do you get your break?"

"Hardly ever."

"Why not?"

"There's too much to do. There's not enough time or energy."

"*You* don't have enough time or energy, but how about the rest of them?"

"Well, they do pitch in. They help."

"Willingly? Frequently? Regularly?"

"No, but they do help."

"Maybe they ought to be helping more, and maybe you ought to program in some regular recreation for yourself. Maybe some of those demands could go unmet."

We could go on, but I think you get the point. This mother's anger was not inappropriate. She was responding to continued pressure from her family.

Pressure that needed to be dealt with not only by saying "Yes," but also by saying "No," or "It's your turn to do it." Her feeling of chronic anger was not a signal of mental illness or sinfulness, but a signal that some new action was called for.

Many of our feelings, particularly our negative feelings, can serve this same purpose for us. They can be used as warning signals that ought to be attended to and understood if we are going to live healthier, fuller lives.

As adults who care about children and their feelings, our first order of business then is to pay attention to our own feelings, explore them, and understand them. We need to do so not only so that we can serve as a model for the children around us, but also so we can be free to be helpful to them. A person who is tied up in emotional knots is of little use to children who are struggling with their own feelings.

Once we have explored, understood, and appropriately dealt with our own feelings, then what? That depends mostly on the age of the child we are attempting to help. In the next few pages we'll be exploring how to help children at various ages deal with their feelings, keeping in mind what has been said about characteristics of children at different levels of emotional maturity.

YOUNG CHILDREN

The young child's primary way to deal with feelings is to *express* them—blatantly, delightfully, and occasionally, painfully. They tend to confuse inner and outer, subjective and objective, and therefore they do not distinguish between their feelings and someone else's feelings, nor between their feelings and objective reality.

A concerned adult rarely has to help a young child express feelings. A young child usually expresses feelings well without any help. In fact, when young children express no feelings—positive or negative—for an extended period of time, it is usually a sign that something is wrong. They may be physically ill, depressed, or simply overwhelmed by a traumatic experience.

One traumatic experience that is difficult for a young child to cope with is that of the death of a family member. Older children understand, at least imperfectly, what it means for someone to die. Young children do not understand "alive" or "dead," and so intellectually they are severely handicapped when it comes to dealing with the death of a loved one. Equally important is the fact that young children cannot *describe* their feelings or *talk about* them, they can only *express* them.

When someone they love dies, children may initially show appropriate feelings; for example, they may cry, or they may have temper tantrums, but they cannot really talk about the way they feel about losing someone they love.

Perhaps the most important role an adult can play to a young child who has lost a sibling, parent, or grandparent is to try to put into words what they think the child might be feeling.

"I know you miss grandma. I do too. I miss being able to go to see her and talk to her on the phone."

"And her apple pies."

"Yes, and her apple pies. She baked them because she loved us."

"But if she loves us, why did she go away?"

"Grandma had to go away. She didn't die because she stopped loving us. It was her time to die. She didn't stop loving you and me. It's just that she can't be here any more."

"Can I see her next week?"

"No. I know it's hard for you to understand that you can't see her any more, but we'll still remember her, and we'll still love her."

The other role that an adult can serve with a young child is to accept the expression of their feelings and then to help them to begin to distinguish and discriminate different ways of expressing their feelings: "I know you're angry at me for not taking you to grandma's. I know that you don't really understand that grandma isn't there any more, but you can't kick me." Or, "I know you're angry. If you have to lie on the floor and scream for awhile, that's OK, but I'm going out in the kitchen because the noise hurts my ears."

Allowing a young child to express feelings does not mean that the adults in the child's life should open themselves to abuse. Let your child express feelings, but protect yourself and others both for your sake and the child's.

It's not always easy to figure out what young children are feeling, or why they're feeling the way they are. But even if you're not blessed with the ability to get inside the world of young children, you can help them find appropriate ways to express their feelings.

There are times when adults, particularly parents, are told by experts: "Let your child express his feelings." Now that's excellent advice, particularly if you're the expert and don't have to live with the child. The expression of feelings is a highly desirable skill for a child to learn, but like any skill, it calls for refinement and nurturing. The screaming tantrum of a two-year-old is no longer tolerable at age five. The biting of the toddler may feel wonderful to his gums, but it is excruciating to the person whose finger is being gnawed on.

Allow, and even help, your young children to express their feelings, but set limits on that expression. Help them to use words rather than teeth, intense voices rather than ear-piercing ones, facial expressions rather than fists. Unexpressed feelings can cause trouble, but so can unsocialized ones.

The main role we adults have with the young child then is *to help them find acceptable ways to express their feelings*—simple in concept, yet not always too easy in practice.

If you survive your young child's growing up—and anyone who has lived through the first five years of a child's life knows they are delightful as well as difficult years—there is another series of challenges and joys in helping the older child tell us how he feels.

As children move into elementary school, they

add to the ability to *express* their feelings, the further ability to *describe* those feelings.

SCHOOL-AGE CHILDREN

School-age children gain some distance from their feelings. They not only express their feelings, but they also recognize that their feelings can be *talked about* in addition to, or instead of, simply being *expressed*.

At this level of development children can describe how they feel about things or people:

"I like that."

"I want that."

They can distinguish between themselves and their own feelings and what is outside them. However, they still locate the feeling outside themselves.

"You made me angry."

"That made me happy."

While an adult can rephrase such statements as the above, "You're angry because . . ." or "You're happy because . . . ," it is unlikely that the young school-age child will really catch the distinction between what they have said and what the adult is saying. It is only in later childhood that children begin to recognize not only that they *have* feelings, but that no one else is responsible for making them feel any particular way.

The distinction between "You made me angry" and "I'm angry," may seem a small one, but it is a very important distinction. If you make me angry, then it's up to you to do something to change the situation. If I'm angry, then it's up to me to take the initiative so that we can work out a solution together.

Helping older school-age children not only to describe how they feel, but to see who or what is responsible for how they feel, can be a difficult but worthwhile undertaking. I'd suggest that you not invest too much energy in the task until the end of the elementary years. Before that time the school-age child simply doesn't have the cognitive tools to make the distinction.

During the early school years, say between the ages of five and ten, the role of the adult is partially a carry-over from the preschool period. We still need to remind the school-age child that there are appropriate and inappropriate ways to express feelings. We need to continue to provide a model of how a feeling is appropriately expressed. Yelling, "Don't hit your brother," while we smack them is not likely to reduce the physical expression of their anger. So a continued good model is still important during the school years.

In addition to continuing to show children how to *express* feelings by doing it ourselves, we can also serve as a model for *describing* feelings: "I'm angry at you for hitting your brother," spoken in a firm angry voice, not only serves as a disciplinary measure; it allows us to show a child how to express and describe feelings.

If school-age children seem stuck in their ability to express a particular feeling, frequently all that is necessary is to provide some private time. Getting away alone with a child and really listening to him is often all that is needed to help the school-age child describe what he is feeling.

If, on the other hand, school-age children seem unable to express or describe their feelings, or a particular type of feeling, it may be because you are subtly telling them not to. If your school-age children can't express affection, it may be because you have difficulty with it, too. If your school-age children can only express anger physically rather than describe their angry feelings, it might be because they see that same behavior in you or in someone else they look up to.

When your school-age children seem unable to express or, more importantly, describe a feeling, try time alone with them. If that doesn't work, check out your own reaction to the feeling they seem stuck on, and chances are pretty good you're stuck on it too. And as Jesus said, "Don't try to pull something out of anyone else's eye until your own vision is clear."

School-age children present challenges, but they also are an opportunity for joy. They no longer bubble the way younger children do, but their ability to describe their own feelings and their insights into other people's can be delightful. Their fresh use of words, and their keen observations can be both funny and wise.

When my twelve-year-old son's team lost a baseball game by a lopsided score, I asked him how he felt about the game. He responded, "That's a good game to forget." No despair, no excuses, just a desire to put it behind him and look toward the next game.

Our school-age children not only have things to learn from us about expressing and describing feelings, we also can be on the receiving end of some of their insights.

Children, like grass in the rain, keep growing. The bubbling preschooler turns into the more staid elementary school child; the child becomes the adolescent.

As children approach adolescence, they often become somewhat more difficult for the adults around them to cope with. Part of that difficulty is because some of the volatileness of early childhood returns. The adolescents' moods change rapidly, and their feelings are once again expressed with bluntness, even crudity.

ADOLESCENTS AND THEIR FEELINGS

The big difference between young children and adolescents is that adolescents have several options open to them. Young children can either *express* or *not express* their feelings. Adolescents, however, can *express, describe,* or *explain* and *compare* the feelings that they have. With all of these additional skills at their disposal, why then do adolescents present such problems for the adults around them, especially their parents?

Perhaps one of the greatest frustrations of parenthood is that adolescents don't talk to their parents about feelings very often. Young children and

school-age children let their parents know how they feel; teenagers usually don't.

While many experts have encouraged parents to talk with their adolescent children about their children's feelings, I personally think that such an endeavor is doomed to fail. It fails not because parents don't try, but because adolescents don't want to share their feelings with their parents.

In our society, the major task of adolescence is to break away from one's family and begin to establish a life of one's own. The place that most adolescents start is with their own feelings.

As children move into adolescence, they become more private. Nor should we be surprised, for what is more private, more personal, more one's own than one's feelings? Fortunately, most adolescents find other people to talk with about their feelings— friends, extended family members, other adults, or even a diary.

My own opinion is that adults, particularly parents, ought to respect the privacy of their adolescent children and not try to force them to talk about how they feel. The one area where I would make an exception is where the adolescent's feelings, particularly *expressed* feelings, have a direct impact on the rest of the family. Then the ability of an adolescent to compare and explain his feelings can be very helpful to everyone involved.

"No! you can't smack your younger brother! Now what's going on?"

"He's always butting in. Nancy and I want to be left alone, and he keeps sticking his face in the door and bothering us. I know I'm not supposed to hit him, but he makes me so angry when he gets that smirk on his face."

"OK, I know he can be a pest, but you know I don't want you smacking your brother. How else do you think you might handle him?"

Such situations call for adult intervention and the working out of a solution, and the finding of a solution involves being clear about how everyone feels. But, whenever possible, I leave my own adolescent children alone as much as possible, not because I don't care about them, but because I respect their privacy and their need to develop a life of their own.

There are times when adolescent children will initiate an exchange of feelings with their parents, and those times are delightful. But, with the exception of crises, these exchanges ought to be initiated by the adolescent and the adolescent ought to control the depth of the interchange.

At times adolescents are able to talk about their feelings in considerable depth, but they have only recently learned to swim. As parents, don't force them into deep water. Let them get there when they're ready. It'll be better for everyone.

THE YOUNG ADULT

One of the potential joys of parenthood is the opportunity to reestablish a relationship with one's own child after that child is grown. Then the relationship is one of equality, because the child has become an adult, established their own right, secure and able to be involved again with parents.

Remember that young adults can explore their feelings, and occasionally, if you are fortunate, they will do that with you. When that happens, the opportunity is present for a delightful experience, the opportunity to chronicle the growth of your child.

"I'm not sure, Dad. I've been thinking about graduate school for a while now, but every time I do, I get a queasy feeling in my stomach. It's like I felt the first time I played ball with someone watching. Maybe I'm afraid I'd fail, that I won't be as smart as the rest of the kids, that I can't make the grade. No, I don't really think that's it. I've gone to a good college. My grades have been good. Somehow that doesn't feel like the issue."

"Any idea what else it might be?"

"I think it has something to do with you."

"Me?"

"Yes, I think so."

"That I wouldn't care for you if you didn't make it?"

"No, that you wouldn't love me if I did."

"That I wouldn't love you if you got into graduate school and did well?"

"Yes, I think that's what I'm scared of. I hadn't realized it before, but I think that's what it is."

"Why would you be afraid of that?"

"Because you never made it through college. You had to quit to go to work. And, I don't know, maybe you'd be envious."

"Envious? Oh, maybe a little, but mostly I'd be proud. I hope you'll do it. I really hope you will."

JODY REVISITED

We've talked about feelings and how children develop the ability to understand and handle them. We've talked about how we adults can help them do that. But we ought to end where we started. Remember Jody, the young boy we met at the beginning of the book? Suppose we return to him ten years later and listen in on another conversation between him and his mother.

"It's time for me to go, Mom. I wish you'd come live with us."

"No, Jody. This is my home. This is where I belong."

"But you know Carol loves you almost as much as I do. It wouldn't be any trouble. We have an extra bedroom."

"I know, Jody. I know."

"Are you sure that Mr. Welmore'll keep an eye on things here?"

"Yes, Jody. He's a good farmer. He's already got all the fields planted. I've known him for years. I trust him. I'll be all right here."

"You'll write, won't you, Mom? And call if you need us?"

"Yes, I will."

"I love you, Mom."

"And you, Jody, I love you," she said reaching up to hug him.

She watched as Jody drove back down the dirt road, back to rejoin his wife and infant son.

She thought about the tomato patch and that other warm summer day so many years before.

"So proud," she heard herself say. "So proud."